Dear Children

From Little to Grown

Author - Rukayya Zirapur |
Relationship Counselor | Entrepreneur

Dear Children

When I say "Dear Children," I'm speaking to each of you, whether you already have big dreams or are still figuring things out.

You know what? No one is born with a dream in their heart. Dreams grow over time, sparked by excitement, inspiration, and those little moments that make us think, **"Wow, I want that too!"**

Have you ever heard a friend say, ***"Mujhe mummy jaisa banna hai"*** or ***"Main bhaiya ke jese doctor banungi"?*** Maybe someone said, ***"My dad is my superhero, and I just want to be like him."*** So chill and amazing!"

Do you know why they say things like that? It's because someone showed them those dreams. They saw something in their family, friends, or even their heroes that made them believe, "***If I can be like them, I'll be amazing too!"***

But not everyone is lucky enough to see their dreams so clearly. Some people just hope for better days, a better life, or maybe enough money to feel happy. And that's okay too!

Dreams don't come from nowhere. Your experiences shape them, the people you meet, and the moments that make you smile, laugh, or even cry. That's why I want to talk to you about your dreams, whether you already have them or are still waiting for that spark.

This book isn't like anything you have read before. It's not a textbook and is not here to tell you what to do or who to be. Instead, it's your guide to learning the things schools don't always teach.

Dear Children

Each chapter is like a little treasure chest, packed with skills and lessons that will stay with you for life. And to make it even more fun, each chapter has a color:

- **Green for Finance**: How to save, spend, and manage money.
- **Orange for Critical Thinking**: How to ask smart questions and solve problems.
- **Pink for Life Balance**: How to juggle school, fun, family, and yourself.
- **Blue for Emotional Intelligence**: How to understand your feelings and connect with others.
- **Grey for Cherishing Loneliness**: How to be your own best friend.

Sounds serious? Maybe a little. But trust me, these are the lessons that will make life way easier and way more exciting as you grow.

Because one day, when no one else is around, the most important person you'll have is you. Learning to trust yourself, understand the world, and chase your dreams is the most powerful thing you can do.

So, let's dive in. Are you ready?

Dear Children

Chapter 1 - Green

Finance: The Magic of Money

PAISA!!!

The coin and the notes that we beg for from our Parents just so we can go out with our friends, right?

'Mamma, Tasneem is going out with Sakina because her mother gave her 100 rupees. They will be partying in the evening, and I will be sitting in Idol.' Isn't that exactly how we try to manipulate our parents into giving us Money? It Sounds like we are 'Bicharas' who can't go out and enjoy ourselves with friends because my Mother is too Strict.

But have you ever thought about money differently? How to earn it, then save it, and make it grow? If not, this is your chance to learn all about Finance!

I remember having a super cool piggy bank where I would put my cash. But as it grew or got better, my parents would use it all.

Every Time I questioned, I wouldn't get my answers. You must have one too where you save your little coins or drop cash like a tradition.

But have you ever wondered what happens to that money or how can it work for you?

Dear Children

We can try to connect it with a little story of a girl named Rosie. She loved saving money in her piggy bank without knowing that money could actually overflow her little savings bank.

So one day, her mom decided to teach her about banking and advised her to open a special account at the bank. Her mom explained that the bank would help her save money and even grow by adding extra cash over time. Rosie was stoked!

But then, she started to get curious... She wanted to know how the bank makes my money grow. What's the secret?

Now even you must be wanting to know the secret, right?

Well, when you put your money in a bank, it's like planting a seed in the ground. Over time, that seed grows into a beautiful flower. That's kinda what happens to your money when you put it in a bank!

The bank uses your money to help other people achieve their goals in the name of a **Loan**, like buying a house or starting a business. And as a thank you, the bank gives you some extra money, called **Interest**.

It's like getting some free money just to keep your cash in the bank. Isn't that awesome? (***But not everyone likes accepting the Interest given for Free***). In Islam, it is certainly Haram (If you are a Muslim child reading this you can discuss it with your Parents and the reason behind it they will be able to help you better).

Dear Children

Now, when you open an account and start saving the cash, it becomes important to manage it well and budget the expenses to make savings work for you.

But wait, do you know what budgeting is?

It's an act to manage money well! It's a smart way to ensure you have enough cash for both the things you need and the things you want.

Supposedly you have 100 rupees in your pocket. You can either use it to buy candy and toys or save it for something special. But how do you decide what to do at the moment?

That's where budgeting comes in! It's like making a money management plan. Where you decide how much you want to spend, save, and give to others.

To connect with this, let's play a game!

Imagine we are a family. I give you 100 rupees as a token of love, and you want to buy some candy and a new toy from it. But you also want to save some money for a new bike.

So what would you do that helps you spend on candies yet helps you save a bit?

You will make a budgeting plan!

Here's an example:

Candy: 20 rupees
Toy: 30 rupees

Dear Children

Savings: 50 rupees

This way you will be able to spend some money on fun things, and also save some for your future goal of buying a new bike.

There are certain ways to make budgeting plans. For now, you can use a book and pen. Make a table with columns and rows and write your budgeting plan. Then keep track of it regularly.

You can also use sticky notes and put them on your favorite wall or wardrobe door.

And of course, that is called the Magic of Saving!

With budgeting, you will encourage monthly savings which will help you buy a new bike you have been craving so much.

So if you wish to buy this bike real soon and within a budget of Rs. 5000/-, you may have to follow the following saving plan:

1. Weekly savings: 500 rupees
2. Number of weeks: 10 weeks

In just 10 weeks, you will have enough money to buy that bike of your dreams!

But honestly, saving is not that easy. You may need to control some of your desires to achieve your dream. It takes hard work, discipline, smart management, and a never-give-up mindset.

Dear Children

For you, the bike may be the biggest achievement right now. But as you grow, you'll realize that saving for your dreams and independence is much more important than the little amount of money you have today.

Now that the topic is getting interesting, I would really like to introduce you to three incredible individuals who never gave up, especially when it came to finance, freedom, and independence.

The Amazing Warren Buffett!

Warren Buffett loved numbers and money. He grew up in Omaha, Nebraska, with big dreams. His family didn't have much money when he was young. Even his dad, who was a stockbroker, was struggling with slow business. Warren wanted to help, so he started selling lemonade, newspapers, and even gum.

Warren always worried that he wouldn't have enough money to buy the things he wanted. So, he made a plan. He saved every single rupee he earned and invested it wisely.

Over time, he created a budget to track every penny he was earning. He divided his money into three jars: one for saving, one for spending, and another for giving.

Warren's saving habits helped him achieve his goals. He bought his first stock at the age of 11! He still lives in the same house he bought in 1958 for $31,500. Warren Buffett is known for his love of Coca-Cola and eats McDonald's for breakfast.

Madam C.J. Walker: The Hair Care Queen

Dear Children

Madam C.J. Walker was an African American entrepreneur who built a hair care empire. Born in 1867, she became one of the wealthiest self-made women of her time. Orphaned at age 7 and raised in poverty, she worked as a laundry woman before becoming a sales agent for a hair care company. However, she soon realized the products didn't work well for African American hair.

Determined to find a solution, Madam Walker created her own line of hair care products, including shampoos, conditioners, and hair growth treatments. She traveled across the country, selling her products and teaching women how to care for their hair.

Her business employed thousands of African American women, helping them achieve financial independence. Madam Walker also donated to charities and supported African American organizations.

Her legacy continues to inspire entrepreneurs and women worldwide. She became the first self-made female millionaire in America and established a beauty school and training program for African American women.

Savitribai Phule: The Education Champion

Savitribai Phule was a pioneering social reformer and educator from India. Born in 1831, she fought for women's rights and education. Savitribai was married at the age of 9 to Jyotirao Phule, a social reformer. **Despite**

facing many challenges, Savitribai became one of the first women teachers in India.

Savitribai believed that education was the key to financial independence and empowerment. She encouraged women to start small businesses, like selling vegetables or flowers, to earn their own income. She also started a school for girls, which was a revolutionary idea at that time.

Savitribai's work has inspired generations of women to fight for their rights, education, and financial independence. She proved that with determination and hard work, anyone can achieve financial freedom.

Now that we have learned some lessons about financial freedom and independence from great personalities, we must remember the significance of making informed decisions about earning money.

Not only informed decisions but also perseverance, determination, and prudent decision-making are essential for achieving financial freedom.

However, some individuals may attempt to take shortcuts or employ dishonest means to acquire wealth.

We usually encounter advertisements or social media posts promising unrealistic financial gains or "easy money" opportunities. These offers may seem appealing, but they often involve hidden risks or consequences.

Dear Children

For instance, some people may try to generate income through network marketing schemes that promise unusually high returns for minimal effort. However, these schemes frequently require substantial investments in products or recruitment of others, which can be unsustainable and potentially harmful.

Others may attempt to earn money by selling counterfeit or low-quality products online or in person. This can damage their reputation and relationships with others.

These practices teach us to always be careful. It's very normal for such people to attract children and college-going students into Easy money-making schemes. That's why we should always prioritize carefulness, honesty, and fairness in our financial decisions.

Now, let's engage in an activity!

Activity Time!

Imagine you are put into the following situations:

1. A friend comes up with a **"get rich quick"** scheme with minimal investment but unbelievable returns. How will you respond?

2. You come across an advertisement on social media that requires 1-2 hours daily **to earn 30-50k monthly**. What questions will you ask before getting involved?

3. A family member **asks your mom** to assist them in selling counterfeit products online. What will you say?

Take a few minutes to think over these situations and discuss them with your classmates or family members.

And that's it for the Finance Chapter! You didn't only learn about the concepts of finance, but also budget management, and saving ideas.

Remember, managing your money isn't like eating a toffy, but surely some powers not everyone can acquire. You can use it to achieve your goals, make your dreams come true, help your families in need, and whatnot!!

It does bring Happiness for sure.

So, What's Next?

In the next chapter, we will learn Critical Thinking. You will learn how to brainstorm and the scope of it in your life. It does wonders when you have the ability to think critically in situations and places that need it the most. And I have compiled some amazing facts and activities for your entertainment.

Well, till then it's your Turn!

Fun Activities!

1. Create a piggy bank or a savings jar to start collecting your coins and cash.

2. Draw a picture of your dream goal, and write down how much money you need to save to achieve it. Try a vision board actually.
3. Play a game with your friends or family members to practice budgeting and saving.

Well, I hope you had fun reading this chapter :) See you in the next chapter!

Chapter 2 - Orange

Critical Thinking - Making Smarter Choices

Have you ever paused for a moment and asked yourself, ***"Is this the best option?"*** Maybe yes, maybe not.

Especially when deciding what to spend your pocket money on or finding the solution to a tricky question at school.

That's what we call critical thinking. A simple yet powerful way to approach problems and decisions.

What is Critical Thinking?

Critical thinking is about using your mind to understand a situation, weigh your options, and make decisions that matter. It's about asking yourself the right questions, looking around for facts, and imagining the bigger picture before jumping to conclusions.

Let's take an example: Your best friend wanted to buy a pair of shoes she saw online on her Father's Mobile Phone. But before clicking "**Buy Now**," her father asked her to think about it.

1. **Do I really need this?**
2. **Is there a better deal elsewhere?**
3. **Will this affect my budget for the month?**

After thinking about her Father's way of thinking and doing some research, she found the same shoes at a lower price and within her budget. That's critical thinking- pausing, assessing, and then acting.

Why Does Critical Thinking Matter?

Critical thinking is essential for several reasons. Let's break it down:

1. Better Decisions

Imagine standing at a crossroads with multiple paths. Critical thinking acts like a map, guiding you toward the path that leads to your goal. Whether it's deciding how to spend your money, solving a tricky math problem, or choosing what to focus on, critical thinking helps you make smarter, well-thought-out decisions.

2. Avoiding Mistakes

It's easy to get carried away and make choices that seem good at the moment but turn out to be wrong later. For example, imagine you spent all your savings on something unnecessary that either breaks after a week or isn't even in use for months. Thinking critically helps you pause and ask, **"Is this toy worth it?"** The habit can save you from regret.

3. Learning More

When you ask questions and explore different possibilities, you understand things more deeply. For instance, instead of memorizing facts for a test, you can ask yourself **"Why is this true?"** That will help you grasp the concept better and remember it for longer.

4. Solving Problems

Life is full of challenges, big and small. Critical thinking equips you with tools to break down problems, analyze them, and find effective solutions. Whether it's fixing a broken gadget or resolving a disagreement with a friend, this skill is invaluable.

How to Think Critically

Now that we know why critical thinking is important, let's explore how to develop it. Here are some practical steps:

1. Ask Questions

The very first step in critical thinking is to be always curious. Whenever you face a situation, start by asking questions. Here are some examples:

- **Why is this happening?**
- **How does this work?**
- **What if I try something different?**

For example, if someone offers you a deal that sounds too good to be true, think, **"Why are they offering this? What's in it for them?"** These questions help you uncover hidden details.

2. Gather Information

Don't rush into decisions. Take some time to collect facts, listen to others, and read up on the topic. Let's say you want to buy a new dress. Before deciding, you could:

- Read reviews online to see what others think about that dress.
- Compare prices at different stores to find the best deal.
- Ask friends if you wish in case they have made any online purchases lately for their experience.

The more information you have, the better your decision will be.

3. Look at All Sides

Every decision has pros and cons. Review them carefully before deciding. For instance, imagine you're planning to spend your pocket money on snacks for a party. The pros are that you'll have fun and impress your friends. The cons are that you'll have less money for other things. Considering both sides helps you make a balanced choice.

4. Consider the Consequences

Think about what might happen if you make a particular choice. Will it help you achieve your goals? Will it create problems later? For example, if you skip studying for a test to watch a movie, the immediate consequence is entertainment, but the long-term consequence might be a poor grade. Understanding these outcomes can guide you toward better decisions.

5. Think Long-Term

Dear Children

Sometimes, it's tempting to choose the easiest or most fun option at the moment. Critical thinking helps you look beyond the present and consider the future. For example, saving money instead of spending it all now can help you buy something more meaningful later.

6. Test Your Ideas

Once you've thought of a solution, test it out. If it doesn't work, don't be discouraged. We certainly learn from our experiences and we must try a different approach next time. This trial-and-error method helps us grow and improve.

Learning from Examples

Ratan Tata: A Visionary Leader

Ratan Tata is one of India's most admired business leaders, known for his thoughtful decisions and deep commitment to helping people. He led the Tata Group, a company involved in everything from cars to steel to tea.

One of his most famous decisions was launching the Tata Nano, a car designed to be affordable for families who couldn't afford traditional cars. The idea came from observing a father and son riding a small scooter, struggling to stay safe in the rain. Ratan Tata thought critically about how to make a safe and affordable car for families. After considering the challenges of cost, manufacturing, and safety, the Tata Nano was born.

Even though the Nano didn't become a massive success, it showed how thinking deeply about a problem and prioritizing people over profits can lead to meaningful innovations. His thoughtful approach teaches us the importance of understanding the needs of others and working toward solutions.

Marie Curie: The Persistent Scientist

Marie Curie was a scientist from Poland who made incredible discoveries about radiation. Her work led to breakthroughs in medicine, including cancer treatment. But her journey wasn't easy.

At a time when women weren't allowed to attend many universities, Marie moved to France to study. She worked tirelessly, often in cold, unheated labs, to uncover the secrets of elements like radium and polonium. She asked questions no one else dared to ask and tested her ideas over and over until she found answers.

Marie's dedication to science earned her two Nobel Prizes - one in Physics and another in Chemistry. Her ability to think critically and persist despite challenges is an inspiration to all of us.

Practice Critical Thinking

Let's try some situations:

1. Your friend offers you a deal where you invest some money, and they promise to double it in a month. What would you do?
2. You have 100 rupees to spend. Do you buy snacks for the day, or save up for a book you've been wanting?

3. A video online claims something shocking but provides no evidence. How do you decide if it's real or fake?

Discuss these scenarios with your friends or family. Think carefully before deciding and explain why you made your choice.

Building a Habit

Critical thinking isn't something you do once; it's a habit you build. The more you practice, the better it will make you. It helps you in your studies, relationships, and even managing your money.

Well, in the next chapter, we will learn all about Balancing Life: how to juggle responsibilities, fun, and personal growth without feeling overwhelmed. Although you are too young for words like responsibilities and growth, it is very important to be able to break down your responsibilities as per your age and situation and understand them.

For now, you have the responsibility to shape your life through your school learnings and examinations. Just like that, you will have different responsibilities as you age.

For now, try to observe how often you make decisions and ask yourself if you have thought about them carefully. With time, it will become second nature.

Chapter 3 - Pink

Balancing Life

Life is like a seesaw!

You have to keep balancing it so that one side doesn't tip over. You also know that if you stand on one end of a seesaw while your best friend is on the other and one of you jumps off or leans too far, the balance will be gone. The seesaw will tip over.

Similarly, in life, if you focus too much on one thing - like playing games all day or gossiping or only studying then you can lose balance.

Have you seen a juggler in the circus, tossing multiple balls in the air? They can keep all the balls moving because they have learned how to pay attention to each one without dropping it.

Balancing life works the same way; with practice, you can make time for everything you enjoy while also taking care of your responsibilities.

At your age, balancing life means juggling school, fun, family, and hobbies. It might feel tricky now, but don't worry, it's a skill you can master. We gotta go one step at a time!

Why Balance Is Important

If you spend all your time playing and forget about school, you might struggle with your studies. If you only study and never take breaks, you might feel too tired to enjoy your favorite things.

Balance keeps you happy, healthy, and focused. It helps you grow into a person who can handle challenges while still having fun.

Identifying Your Responsibilities

Let's start by figuring out what responsibilities you have. Here are a few examples:

1. **School:** Your biggest responsibility right now is to do your best at school. This includes attending classes, doing homework, and preparing for tests.
2. **Home:** Maybe you help out at home, like cleaning your room, feeding a pet or even looking after your younger siblings.
3. **Friendship:** Being a good friend means making time to play and talk with others while being kind and supportive.
4. **Self-love:** Taking care of your health, eating well, and getting enough sleep are also important responsibilities. You are what you eat and think so never stop looking after your needs.

Write down your responsibilities in a notebook. For example, you could create a simple table with two columns: one for the responsibility (like 'Homework') and the other for how often you need to do it (like

'Daily'). Or, you can draw pictures to represent your responsibilities if you enjoy being creative! This will help you see what you need to balance.

Making Time for Fun

While responsibilities are important, so is fun! Fun gives your brain a break and keeps you motivated. Think about the activities you enjoy the most. Is it playing football, drawing, reading, gaming, or maybe just talking?

Make sure you set aside time for these things every day.

Creating a Schedule

One of the best ways to balance life is to make a simple schedule. Here's how:

1. **List Everything:** Write down your responsibilities and fun activities.
2. **Set Priorities:** Decide which things are most important. For example, what might come before watching a movie?
3. **Plan Your Day:** Create a daily routine. For example:
    - Morning: School
    - Afternoon: Homework
    - Evening: Playtime
    - Night: Family time and bedtime

Sticking to a routine will make balancing easier.

Dealing with Overwhelm

Dear Children

Sometimes, even with a schedule, life can feel too busy. When that happens:

1. **Take a Break:** It's okay to pause and relax for a while. You can also try to have conversations with your siblings or grandparents.
2. **Ask for Help:** Talk to a parent, teacher, or friend if you're feeling stressed. They can help you figure out what to do.
3. **Do One Thing at a Time:** Instead of worrying about everything, focus on finishing one task before moving to the next. We always climb step by step and not jump to the destination.

Fun Activity: Create Your Balance Wheel

1. Draw a big circle on a piece of paper.
2. Divide it into sections for school, home, friends, fun, and self-care. For example, you can color each section differently to make it more fun.
3. In each section, either write or draw activities or tasks you do. For example, in the "school" section, you could draw a book or write "homework."
4. Check if any section is too full or too empty. If your "fun" section has fewer things than "school," think about adding more activities to balance it out.

Try this: Add stickers, drawings, or even cut-out pictures from magazines to make your balance wheel look creative and exciting. You can also hang it on your wall as a reminder to stay balanced!

Dear Children

Well, Did you know that even adults struggle to balance their responsibilities? If you see a chef in a busy kitchen. They don't only have to cook multiple dishes at the same time, but also make sure nothing burns, and plate everything perfectly. It can get overwhelming, but they succeed by staying organized and focused.

Just like that chef, you can learn to manage your responsibilities while keeping calm and enjoying the process. That's why it's so important to practice balance while you are young. The earlier you start, the better you will get at it!

Questions to Think About

1. What are your top three responsibilities right now?
2. How much time do you spend having fun each day?
3. What changes can you make to balance your time better?

Fun Facts

Tom and Jerry: Have you ever noticed how Jerry plans carefully to outsmart Tom? Whether he is gathering cheese or escaping a tricky trap, Jerry always tries to balance fun with staying alert. Just like Jerry, you can find a balance between focus and fun in life!

Shinchan: Shinchan loves playing and joking around, but he also helps his parents and friends whenever they need him. Life isn't all play or work, but also about doing a little of both.

Dear Children

In the next chapter, we will explore another important skill to help you grow and succeed. Until then, keep practicing your balance, and don't forget to have fun!

Chapter 4 - Blue

Emotional Intelligence

Have you ever heard of someone named *Barack Obama*? He was the President of the US (United States), and one of the things people admire about him was his ability to stay calm and make smart decisions, even during tough days.

Barack Obama was really good at understanding his own emotions. He could also understand the feelings of others. In fact, his ability to manage his emotions and understand those of other people around him helped him become a great leader.

But you know what? You don't have to be a president to have emotional intelligence!

Emotional intelligence, or *EQ*, is something we all have. But we forget to realize the exact use of it. If you cannot understand and manage your own emotions. You will certainly not be able to understand others.

So, what exactly is emotional intelligence, and why is it so important?

What Is Emotional Intelligence?

Emotional intelligence is the ability to recognize and understand your own emotions, as well as the emotions of those around you. It's about managing these emotions and using them to communicate effectively, connect with others, and make thoughtful decisions.

In fact, not only communicate well, but also listen well.

People with high EQ are able to stay calm under pressure, handle their feelings in healthy ways, and understand what others are going through.

The better they are able to understand their inner emotions, the better they are able to understand the outer emotions of other people.

This amazing ability helps you have a greater bond with yourself, your friends, your family, and future relationships.

When you will grow up into an adult, you will go through phases. From a basic happy phase to difficult crying situations. That's where your emotional intelligence will help you sort your life well if you put some effort into improving it today!

There are five main parts of emotional intelligence:

Self-Awareness: This means understanding your own emotions. For example, if you feel nervous before a test or excited about seeing your best friend, self-awareness helps you recognize and name what you're feeling. When you can name your emotions, it's easier to handle them.

Self-Regulation: This ability helps you manage your emotions, especially when you're upset or angry. Self-regulation helps you stay calm, think before you act, and make better decisions. It's like checking in the "pause" button just when you are about to do something that you might regret later.

Motivation: Emotional intelligence also helps you stay motivated to reach your goals. Whether you want to learn a new skill, finish your homework, or even get better at a sport, motivation is what pushes you to keep going, even when things get tough.

Empathy: Empathy is the ability to understand how other people are feeling. It's about putting yourself in someone else's shoes and recognizing their emotions. If a friend is sad or worried, empathy helps you know how to support them.

Social Skills: These are the skills that help you interact well with others. Whether it's about making friends, working in a group, or solving conflicts, social skills are key to building strong relationships and getting along with people.

Why Does Emotional Intelligence Matter?

Now that we know what emotional intelligence is, you must know, *Why does it matter?* And that is because it can help you in so many areas of life, from school to friendships, to your future career in whatever profession you admire to achieve.

Let's take a look at how EQ can make a difference:

Better Friendships: When you understand your own emotions and can read the emotions of others, it helps you connect better with them. You can tell when they are happy, sad, or worried, and you know the best way to support them. This helps you form stronger, healthier friendships.

Handling Tough Situations: Life isn't always easy. Sometimes you may feel a pile of emotions. Emotional intelligence helps you handle those feelings in a healthy way. For example, instead of yelling because you are upset, you will be able to manage it - as you may stop, take a deep breath, and think about what you can do otherwise.

Doing Well in School: When you understand your feelings, it's easier to stay focused and calm during important tests. If you get nervous, emotional intelligence helps you manage that feeling and do your best. In fact, if you're feeling stuck on homework, having a high EQ helps you ask for help or find ways to stay motivated.

Being a Great Leader: Leaders who understand their emotions and the emotions of others can make better decisions, motivate their team, and even build trust. Whether you're leading a group project or helping a friend, emotional intelligence helps you become a better leader.

Fun Facts About Emotions

Before we see how you can build your own emotional intelligence, here are a few cool facts about emotions:

Your brain is always working. When you feel happy, sad, excited, or angry, your brain is sending signals to your body. Like when you feel nervous, your heart might start to race. Understanding how emotions work helps you deal with them better.

Emotions can spread. Did you know that if someone around you is feeling happy, they can pass that happiness to you too? Emotions are contagious. This is why being around positive people can help you feel good about yourself and the environment.

It's okay to feel different emotions. Sometimes people think that certain emotions, like anger or sadness, are bad. But every emotion is important! What really matters is how we choose to react to those feelings. So never listen to anyone coming up to you to tell you that your emotions are invalid, or you are overreacting or overthinking. Every feeling comes from a pile of emotions and everything you feel is just as important as you think.

How to Build Your Emotional Intelligence

The good news is that you can get better at emotional intelligence just like any other skill. The more you put work into it, the easier it gets to understand and manage your emotions. Here are a few ways to improve your emotional intelligence:

Pay Attention to Your Emotions: The first step in building emotional intelligence is to notice what you're feeling. Are you happy, sad, or frustrated? Take a moment each day to check in with yourself and think about how you are feeling. This helps you become more self-aware.

Take a Pause: When you feel any negative emotion, try to pause before reacting. It's easy to say or do things in the heat of the moment that we later regret. Instead of yelling or making a snap decision, take a deep breath, count to 10, and think about how you want to respond.

Put Yourself in Others' Shoes: If you see someone who's upset, try to understand or picture what they might be feeling. Are they sad, frustrated, or worried? Empathy helps you understand others better and show them you care.

Practice Listening: Good communication is key to emotional intelligence. When someone is talking to you, really listen. Don't interrupt and let them finish their thoughts, and then respond. This helps build trust and shows that you care about what they're saying.

Stay Positive: It's easy to get caught up in negative thoughts, especially when things don't go your way. But focusing on the positive side can help you manage your emotions better. Try to find something good in every situation, even when things aren't that perfect.

Activities to Build Your EQ

Want to practice your emotional intelligence? Here are some activities to help you get started:

1. Feelings Check-In

At the end of each day, write down how you're feeling and why. Are you happy, sad, excited, or worried? What caused you to feel that way? This will help you get better at recognizing your emotions and understanding why you feel the way you do.

2. Compliment Someone

Take a moment each day to give someone a compliment. It could be your friend, a teacher, or even a family member. Tell them something you appreciate about them, like their kindness, their hard work, or their smile. Compliments can make people feel happy and strengthen your relationships.

3. Emotion Charades

Want to practice recognizing emotions? Play a game of emotional charades! One person acts out a feeling like happiness, sadness, or surprise and the others have to guess which emotion they're showing. It's a fun way to get better at understanding emotions.

Chapter 5 - The Power of Grey

Cherishing Loneliness

Have you ever noticed the color grey? It's not as bright as white or as dark as black. It's somewhere in the middle - maybe a mix of both?

Some people might call grey a boring color, but do you know what? Grey is special. It's calm, peaceful, and full of possibilities, just like the moments when you're by yourself.

Today, let's talk about something called **"loneliness."** Now, before you think, *"Oh no, this sounds sad!"* hold on.

Loneliness isn't always bad. In fact, if you learn how to cherish it, it can be one of the most magical things in your life.

Why Does Loneliness Feel So Grey?

Loneliness can feel like a grey day. You know, when the clouds cover the sun, and everything looks quiet and still. Some people see those days and think, **"Ugh, how dull!"** But others might see them and think, **"Wow, it's so peaceful."** It's all about how you look at it.

Dear Children

Loneliness might make you feel sad sometimes, and that's okay.

Everyone feels like that once in a while. Even grown-ups! Some days you might feel like you don't have anyone to talk to, or maybe you're missing a friend. But what if I told you that these moments are actually a gift in disguise?

Growing Up Means Facing Grey Days

When you grow up, you will have days that feel lonely. Maybe you will move to a new place where you don't know anyone yet. Or maybe you will have a day when you feel like no one understands you. Some grown-ups call these feelings "sadness" or even "depression."

But guess what? If you learn how to enjoy your own company now, those grey days won't feel so scary later. You will know how to turn them into something beautiful.

The Hidden Treasures of Alone Time

Being alone gives you time to

Get to Know Yourself
Did you know that you are like a treasure chest? When you spend time alone, you can discover all the amazing things about yourself. Just like what you love, what you're good at, and what makes you happy.

Be Creative
Trust me, some of the best ideas come when you are alone or struggling to sleep at night and everything is

just 'SILENT'. Maybe you will end up writing a story, draw a picture, or even build something cool.

If you ask me, I started two of my companies just when I was feeling too alone at night and had no friends to go out with or enjoy Saturday night with.

Now you may think, 'This person is grown up and they also feel alone.' Well yes, we all do. Isn't that the reason why I am willing to help you understand the importance of cherishing loneliness so it doesn't turn into the most difficult phase of your life later?

Fun Things to Do When You're Alone

Here are some cool ideas for your alone time:

- Write a secret journal where you can write your thoughts or dreams.
- Try drawing your "lonely feelings" as a picture.
- Build something with your block games or anything you have.
- Go outside and listen to nature birds chirping, wind blowing, or leaves rustling.
- Create a **"gratitude list"** of all the good things you have done in life.

Talking About Sadness

Sometimes, being alone can feel heavy, like carrying a big backpack. If that happens, it's important to tell someone you trust - a parent, teacher, or friend. Sharing your feelings can make the backpack feel lighter.

But here's the trick: if you practice cherishing loneliness, you'll see it differently. It won't feel like a heavy backpack anymore. It'll feel like a cozy blanket, where you can wrap up yourself in a quiet hug.

The Grey Superpower

Think about superheroes. They often work alone, planning, thinking, and becoming stronger. Your alone time is like your superpower. It's when you become your own best friend.

So the next time you feel lonely, remember: it's not a bad thing. It's just grey, calm, peaceful, and full of possibilities.

Activity Time!

1. **Draw Your Grey Day**: Grab some crayons or pencils and draw what a "grey day" looks like to you. Is it a soft cloudy sky? A quiet park? Make it as beautiful as you want.
2. **The Treasure Hunt**: Write down five things you love about yourself. It could be anything: your kindness, your jokes, your imagination. These are your treasures!
3. **Loneliness Jar**: Find an empty jar and small slips of paper. Every time you feel lonely, write something you're grateful for and put it in the jar. Watch your jar fill up with happy thoughts!

A Secret for the Road

Here's a little secret: some of the world's most creative, courageous, and wise individuals actually treasured their alone time. They didn't view loneliness as something to fear. Instead, they embraced it as a powerful opportunity to grow.

For example, think about **Albert Einstein**, the brilliant scientist who discovered amazing things about how the world works. He often spent hours alone, thinking and dreaming. During these quiet moments, he came up with ideas that changed the world!

Or take **J.K. Rowling**, the author of the amazing Harry Potter books. She wrote her stories during some very lonely and challenging times. But instead of letting those moments bring her down, she turned them into a magical world that millions of people love.

Even artists like **Vincent van Gogh** used their alone time to paint beautiful pictures. His art might not have been appreciated much during his life, but today, people travel worldwide to see his work.

These people didn't run away from loneliness. They embraced it and used it to think, create, and discover who they were. And you can do the same.

The next time a grey moment comes, smile and say, **"Hello, loneliness. Let's make something beautiful together."** Who knows? Maybe one day, your ideas will inspire the world too!

The Last Chapter

Wow, look at you, making it all the way to the last chapter! You've accomplished something amazing by reading this book. But guess what? This isn't the end, it's just the beginning of your LIFE adventure.

We just covered some pretty awesome topics together, didn't we? Like how to save and spend money wisely in the finance chapter. Then, we learned how to think for ourselves in the critical thinking chapter.

We also figured out how to balance all the wild parts of life. From exploring emotional intelligence, we learned ways to understand and manage our feelings like a pro.

And, of course, we discovered that being alone doesn't have to be scary. We can always make it sound beautiful by cherishing it and enjoying our own company.

Why I Wanted to Write This Book for You?

Hey, can I share a little story with you?

When I was your age, I didn't know all these things. No one really talked about them. I had to figure out a lot of it on my own. And let me tell you, it wasn't always easy.

There was a time when I spent all my pocket money on silly things and didn't save a single coin. Later, when I wanted something big, I had no money left! I wished someone had taught me how to save back then.

Or the times when I believed everything people told me without asking questions. I remember getting stuck in some tricky situations just because I didn't stop to think, ***"Wait, does this even make sense?"***

Oh boy, balancing life? That was hard. I would get super busy with one thing, like school or friends, and forget about the other important stuff, like taking care of myself or spending time with family.

And Feelings? I truly struggled there too. Sometimes, I would get upset and not even know why. Other times, I would see a friend feeling sad but not know how to help. Learning about my feelings and those of others was a life-changing event.

I also used to think loneliness was bad, something to run away from. But as I grew older, I learned that being alone could actually be beautiful. It gave me time to dream, create, and just be me.

That's why I wrote this book for you. I don't want you to wait until you're all grown up to learn these things. I wanted to share them with you because they can make life so much easier and more fun later.

What's Next for You?

So, what do you do now? Well, this book isn't about giving you all the answers. It's about helping you start asking the right questions.

Dear Children

There will be times when you remember something we talked about here, like when you're saving for a cool toy or figuring out how to solve a tricky problem. And maybe one day, when you feel sad or lonely, you'll think, **"Hey, I know how to handle this!"** That's when you will realize how much you have grown.

A Few Things I Want You to Remember

Before we wrap this up, here are some last things I want you to keep in your heart:

It's okay to make mistakes. Mistakes are like stepping stones as they help you get to the other side.

Be curious. Ask lots of questions. Never stop wondering how the world works.

Be kind to yourself and others.

You are never alone - Even on tough days, you must choose to love yourself no matter what!

Your Story is Just Starting

Now, it's your turn to take what you have learned and do amazing things in life. Try practicing one lesson at a time and see how it makes you feel.

Thank you for letting me help you with my wisdom and I'm so very proud of you.

So, go out there, be brave, and most importantly, be YOU. The world is waiting for your magic!!!

With lots of love and belief in you,

Dear Children

Your Friend - Rukayya Zirapur

Instagram - @rukayyazirapur & Website - https://rukayya.com

www.ingramcontent.com/pod-product-compliance
Lightning Source LLC
LaVergne TN
LVHW091241150826
845673LV00003B/1243

* 9 7 9 8 8 9 6 7 3 6 9 7 4 *